rit.
a tempo
mp
mf

32
mp
mf
35
mp
38
41
44
rit. e dim.
RH
p

RECITAL SUITE SERIES

Late Intermediate

WEST VIRGINIA: THE MOUNTAIN STATE

Martha Mier

New River Gorge

An Appalachian Ballad

Fiddler's Tune

Alfred

New River Gorge

A rugged, white-water river flowing northward through deep canyons, the New River is among the oldest rivers on the continent. Construction on the New River Gorge Bridge was completed in 1977. This steel bridge, near Fayetteville, was the longest arch bridge in the world for many years (it now is ranked third) and has become a symbol of West Virginia. Visitors to New River Gorge can enjoy white-water rafting, zip-line tours, hiking, and horseback riding while viewing the stunning natural beauty of the gorge.

Copyright © 2011 by Alfred Music Publishing Co., Inc.
All rights reserved. Printed in USA.

An Appalachian Ballad

The people of the Appalachian Mountains are songwriters and storytellers. Traditional Appalachian ballads were songs that told a story and were based mostly on the ballads and folk dance tunes brought to the area by Anglo-Celtic immigrants. These ballads often included tragic stories about a lost love or an unsolved mystery. Lives, emotions, loves, and fears were found in ballads, echoing people's triumphs and sorrows.

Martha Mier

Moderately, with tenderness

13
mf
16
19
poco rit.
a tempo
mp
mf
22

25
28
31
a tempo
poco rit.
mp
34
p
rit.

Fiddler's Tune

The fiddle was the lead instrument in mountain dance music and a good fiddler was a prize in any early West Virginia settlement. As fiddlers played dance tunes influenced by Anglo-Celtic immigrants, the people danced. Clogging was the social dance in the Appalachian Mountains as early as the 18th century. Later, dances such as flat-footing, foot-stomping, buck dancing, and jigging evolved. Today, traditional fiddle tunes still thrive in the remote regions of West Virginia and are considered a national treasure.

Fast, raucously

Martha Mier

17
poco rit.
21
a tempo
mf
25
29

33
f
37
41
mp
45

49
f
53
57
mp
62
f
ff

Alfred's

RECITAL SUITE SERIES was created for performing piano students. Each suite is a short collection of fresh-sounding solos carefully crafted to be played as a group in a recital. Musical challenges, appropriate for the level, provide interest and appeal. Aspiring pianists are challenged to reach higher degrees of excellence while playing music that is truly enjoyable for them and their audiences.

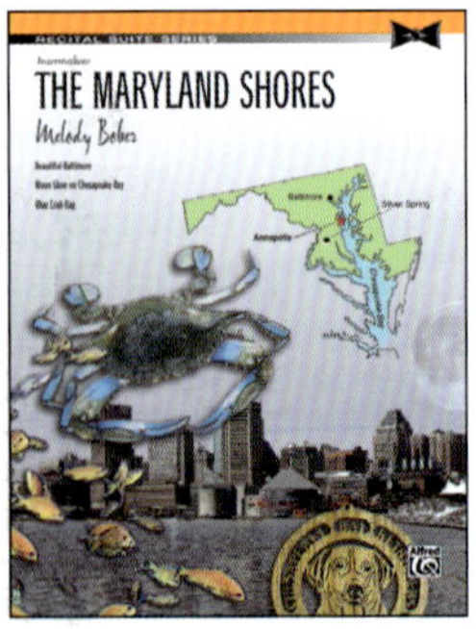

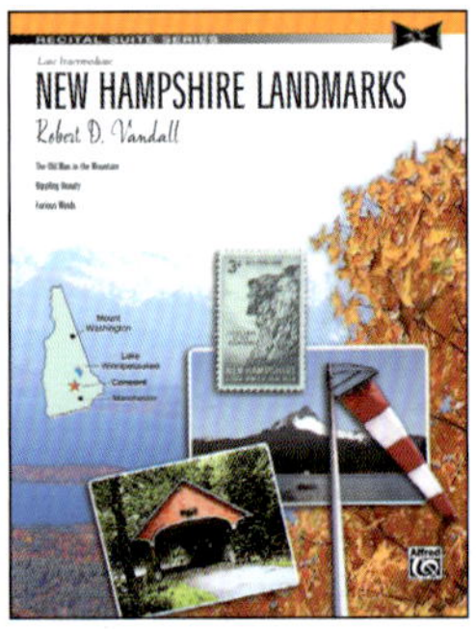

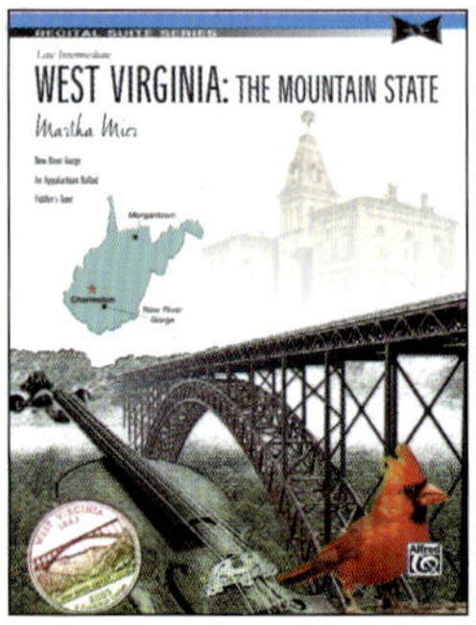

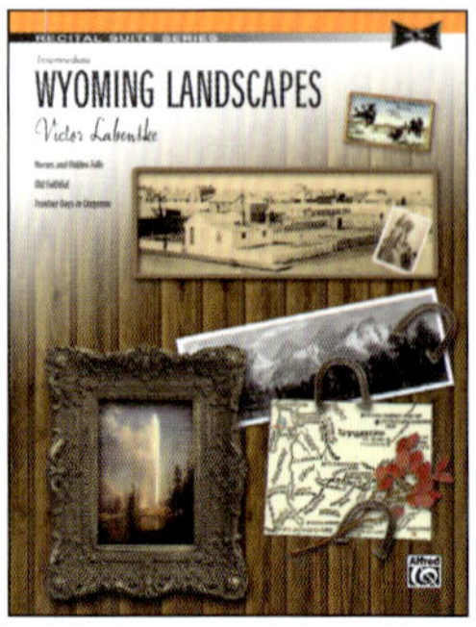

Dennis Alexander
The Carolinas (LI) 33895
The Great Northwest (LI) 23248
Kansas: The Sunflower State (LI) 29167
Scenes from New Jersey (LI) 38796
Vignettes of Hattiesburg (I) 37125

Melody Bober
The Dakotas (LI) 34420
The Great Lakes (LI) 28290
Impressions of Indiana (I) 37126
The Maryland Shores (I) 38794
Postcards from Iowa (LI) 31814
Suite Alabama: A Jazz Sonatina (I) 31464

Dan Coates
Hollywood Dreams (LI) 27714

W. T. Skye Garcia
The Empire State (I) 24544

Tom Gerou
Atlantic Seaboard (LI) 31914
An Australian Journal (I) 21410
California Coastline (LI) 21321

Joyce Grill
Minnesota Moments (I) 26138
Snapshots of Wisconsin (I) 27031

Marilynn Ham
Michigan Images (LI/EA) 22392

Randall Hartsell
Hawaiian Getaway (I) 23266

Andrew Higgins
Three Celtic Legends (LI/EA) 23249

Peter Jancewicz
Sketches of Canada (LI/EA) 22393

Bernadine Johnson
Land of Lincoln (LI) 29100
Nebraska: The Cornhusker State (I) 37127

Gayle Kowalchyk
The Lone Star State (I) 22427
New England Memories (I) 21322

Victor Labenske
Four Corners Suite (I) 22372
Show Me Missouri! (I) 27030
Sounds of Pennsylvania (I) 37128
Wyoming Landscapes (I) 38798

Betty Lea Martocchio
The Connecticut River (I) 37124

Carol Matz
Our Nation's Capital (I) 31813

Martha Mier
Arkansas Suite (I) 20781
The Bluegrass State (LI) 31815
Florida Reflections (I) 22394
Louisiana Legacies (LI) 27028
Tennessee Treasures (LI) 34422
West Virginia: The Mountain State (LI) 38797

Catherine Rollin
The Grand Canyon (I) 34423
Mississippi Moods (I) 21397
Suite Georgia: A Sonatina (LI) 31913

Wynn-Anne Rossi
Along the Mississippi (LI) 34419

Mary K. Sallee
Oklahoma Heritage (LI) 24618

Mike Springer
Alaskan Adventures (I) 29099

Robert D. Vandall
Historic Virginia (I) 28984
Nevada Riches (LI) 27029
New Hampshire Landmarks (I) 38795
Ohio Skylines (LI) 24610
Scenes from the South (EI) 32090

38797 US $4.50
0 38081 42887 1
Alfred
alfred.com
9780739084205
TP APEX